Beginning History

THE GREAT FIRE OF LONDON

Liz Gogerly

Illustrated by Donald Harley

WAYLAND

Published in 2002 by Hodder Wayland,
an imprint of Hodder Children's Books
Reprinted in 2003, 2004 and 2005

Reprinted in 2006, 2007 (twice), 2008 and 2009 by Wayland,
an imprint of Hachette Children's Books

British Library Cataloguing in Publication Data
Gogerly, Liz
The Great Fire of London. - (Beginning History)
1. Great Fire, London, England, 1666 - Juvenile literature
I. Title
942.1'066

ISBN-13: 978 0 7502 3789 5

Printed and bound in China

Wayland
338 Euston Road, London NW1 3BH
Wayland is an Hachette UK Company
www.hachette.co.uk

Picture Acknowledgements
The publishers would like to thank the following for allowing their pictures to be
reproduced in this publication: Mary Evans Picture Library title page, 5, 6, 7, 8, 9,
10, 15 (top and bottom), 20, 22; Private Collection/Bridgeman Art Library 8;
City of Westminster Archive Centre/Bridgeman Art Library 13; Private
Collection/Bridgeman Art Library 16; John Bethell/Bridgeman Art Library 17;
Museum of London back cover, 3, 12, 17, 19; Peter Newark Picture Library 18;
Wayland Picture Library 11, 21; The Imperial War Museum 21.

While every effort has been made to secure permission, in some cases it has
proved impossible to trace copyright holders.

Contents

A Dangerous City

In 1666 London was a lively town. Its narrow streets were filled with thousands of people. Wooden-framed buildings were built high and leaned towards each other over the roads. Houses were sometimes built so close together that it was possible to reach out of a window and shake hands with the person in the house opposite. London was becoming overcrowded yet nobody thought about the risk of fire.

Crowded housing meant that fire was not the only danger that Londoners faced. In 1665 the plague had spread quickly and killed many people.

▼

4

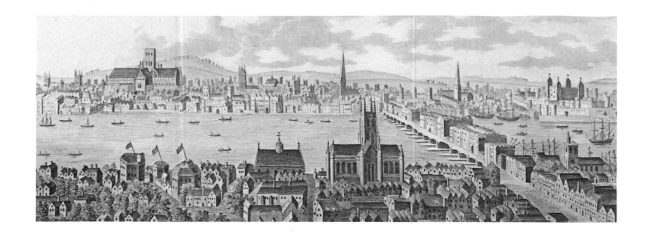

Candles burned and wood or coal fires blazed. Fire was used to cook and keep warm. Tradesmen, such as bakers and blacksmiths, needed fire. London was one great fire hazard but nobody seemed aware of the danger ahead.

▲ A view of London from about 1660. A fire could easily spread from building to building.

London's Burning

The summer of 1666 had been very hot. The houses were dry and a single spark from a fire could set a building ablaze. Early in the morning of Sunday, 2 September, the Great Fire of London leapt into life. Thomas Farryner, a baker in Pudding Lane, had forgotten to sweep out his oven. It caught fire and burned down his shop. Very soon all of Pudding Lane was alight.

▲ A baker makes bread. Thomas Farryner made biscuits for the Navy.

By three o'clock the flames in Pudding Lane could be seen from a quarter of a mile away.
▼

▲ London Bridge had lots of houses built on it, like Nonsuch House. Many were lost to the fire.

The Mayor of London rushed to inspect the fire. A strong wind was driving the fire towards London Bridge. 'It's nothing!' the Mayor said. But already the warehouses along Thames Street were under threat, and the oil and alcohol stored there would feed the greedy fire.

Everybody Out!

By Monday morning the fire was eating its way through the town. Flames had consumed London Bridge and 300 houses had burned down. Samuel Pepys, the famous diarist, was angry when people fled. 'Nobody to my sight endeavouring to quench it, but to remove their goods and leave all to the fire,' he wrote in his diary.

First Pepys buried his best cheese and wine in a box in his garden. Then he visited King Charles II and told him what to do in the crisis. 'Pull down the buildings,' he said. 'Then there shall be gaps which will stop the fire from spreading.' But the King didn't take Pepys' advice and the fire blazed on.

▲ A mother clutches her baby, while the father rescues possessions from the fire.

The Fire Rages

On Monday evening the sky was so bright it looked like day. Ash fell from the burning buildings like snow. On Tuesday the fire was so hot that nobody could get near enough to fight it. Equipment such as wooden ladders, leather buckets, fire-hooks and hand-squirts were no match for the angry flames.

The fire raged in many directions and Pepys organized the demolition of buildings. Many people didn't want their houses to be pulled down, but it was the best way to stop the fire. When St Paul's Cathedral caught fire and Fleet Street was in flames, King Charles II took action. He ordered that more buildings should be demolished.

▲ When old St Paul's Cathedral caught fire, its stone walls soon crumbled.

Some people escaped ▶ the fire by boat, while others got away on carts or on foot.

Fighting the Fire

On Tuesday night the wind that had helped the fire to spread had calmed down. On Wednesday the sound of gunpowder explosions filled the air. People now realized that they must demolish houses and shops in order to save more important buildings such as the Tower of London.

◀ People were pleased that the Tower of London was saved. Some people had taken their money there for safe keeping.

▲ People started to try and fight the fire. The King gave out guineas to encourage workmen to help.

King Charles II didn't mind getting dirty when he was working to put out the fire.
▼

The King himself took charge of fire-fighting in parts of the city. Many people followed the example of their king. Buckets of water were passed along lines of men and thrown on the fire. The biggest flames started to die down. The fire was under control.

The Damage Done

Three days of raging flames had destroyed 400 streets, 13,200 houses and 87 churches. London would never be the same again. Only a handful of buildings and churches remained. St Paul's Cathedral had been badly damaged but it could be rebuilt – together with the rest of the city.

The top picture shows London before the fire. Even though it was overcrowded, London was a beautiful city.

The bottom picture shows London after the fire.

Throughout ▶ the city, buildings were in ruins. Like so many churches and hospitals, this prison at Ludgate was destroyed.

▲ This statue is a memorial of the Great Fire. It was placed at Pye Corner in Smithfield, where the fire ended.

It was a miracle that only nine people had died in the fire. Most people had managed to escape to the fields surrounding the city. Rich and poor people had set up tents and huts beside each other in Moorfields, Highgate and Islington. Pepys was surprised that many rich people had saved their pianos from the fire.

15

Building a New City

King Charles II wanted to build a grand new city. He dreamed of wide streets, great parks and no overcrowding. This dream needed a town plan. Great architects such as Sir Christopher Wren planned a beautiful new city. It would be the envy of all Europe.

▲ **Sir Christopher Wren designed the new St Paul's Cathedral. The building took 44 years to build.**

The Monument to the Great Fire was also designed by Sir Christopher Wren. You can still see the Monument in ▼ London today.

The King's dream never came true. There was neither the time nor the money. Tradesmen needed to get their businesses up and running again. The cheapest and quickest way to rebuild London was for everyone to build their own properties in the same places as before. It would take 30 years to rebuild London properly.

People from other towns sent gifts of money to help rebuild London. This is a receipt for the money sent by the villagers of Cowfold in Sussex.

▼

Making Changes

The Great Fire had scared Londoners. Pepys had nightmares for months afterwards. To prevent such a disaster happening ever again, new rules were made. Buildings were to be made from brick and stone rather than wood. Houses could only be two storeys high in back streets or four storeys high in main streets. They were also built further apart.

This is a seventeenth-century fire-engine. The water tank needed to be topped up with buckets of water so it wasn't very good!
▼

These Engins (which are ___ the best) to quench great Fires; are

◄ One of the first horse-drawn fire-engines rushes to the scene of a fire.

Fire-fighting changed for ever too. New equipment was bought. Each area of London had to have a certain number of buckets, ladders and hand-squirts. Later on, the first horse-drawn fire-engines appeared. Towns all around Britain made sure they were prepared to tackle any fire.

A leather bucket and a hand-squirt of the kind used by London fire fighters in 1666.
▼

London Burns Again

Brick buildings and better fire-fighting mean that London has never known such a disaster again. But London is no stranger to fires either. In 1698, Whitehall Palace burned down. In 1834, the Houses of Parliament were destroyed in a fire. When the Germans bombed London during the Second World War the night skies were once again orange with flames. Thousands of people were killed and their homes were destroyed.

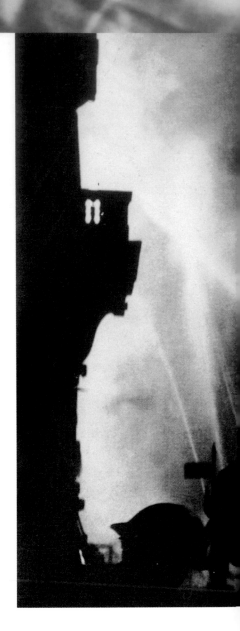

▲ During the Second World War, London fire fighters used powerful hoses to put out the massive fires.

◀ When the Houses of Parliament burned down in 1834, firemen tried to fight the blaze with horse-drawn fire-engines.

In the twenty-first century, the people of London are prepared for fire. Fire alarms let them know when they start and fire-engines rush to put them out. Hopefully, Londoners will never know the destruction of the Great Fire of 1666 ever again.

▲ Despite all the modern equipment, a fire fighter still has one of the most dangerous jobs.

Glossary

Architects People who make plans for buildings.

Blacksmiths People who make things out of iron, such as horseshoes.

Consumed Destroyed so there is nothing left.

Crisis A time of danger.

Demolition The pulling down and breaking up of a building.

Diarist Somebody who regularly writes down things which happen to him or her in a diary.

Endeavouring Trying hard to do something.

Fire alarms Bells which ring as a warning if a fire starts.

Fire hazard A thing which has a high risk of causing fire.

Fire-hooks Poles with a hook on the end. They were used to pull burning roofs off buildings.

Gunpowder A powder which explodes easily when it is set alight. Usually used in old-fashioned guns, bombs or in modern fireworks.

Hand-squirts Early kind of water hoses. The water came from barrels rather than taps.

Quench To put out a fire or cool something down.

Storey One floor of a building. Most houses have two storeys – an upstairs storey and a downstairs storey.

Tradesmen People who practise a particular craft – such as carpentry or weaving.

Warehouses Large buildings where things are stored.

Further Information

Books to Read

Historical Stories: The Great Fire of London by Jill Atkins (Wayland, 2008)

Popcorn: History Corner: Great Fire of London by Jenny Powell (Wayland, 2009)

Ways into History: The Great Fire of London by Sally Hewitt (Franklin Watts, 2004)

Places to Visit

St Paul's Cathedral, St Paul's Churchyard, London EC4 – you can visit the magnificent cathedral designed by Sir Christopher Wren after the fire.

The Monument to the Great Fire, Monument Street, London EC3 – you can climb the tall tower designed by Sir Christopher Wren. The Monument is 61.5 metres high which is the same distance as the Monument is from the shop in Pudding Lane where the fire began.

Pudding Lane, London EC3 – the street looks different today, but you can still find a plaque which shows where the fire started.

St Olave's Church, Hart Street, London EC3 – you can see one of the few churches which survived the fire. Inside the church you can find a memorial tablet for Samuel Pepys.

Index